Biography of
Cole Palmer for
Kids

How a Passion for Football Turned into Stardom

BY KLEIN B. SCOTT

Table of Contents

INTRODUCTION

Welcome to the World of Cole Palmer!

Have you ever dreamed of being a football star? Meet Cole Palmer, a young footballer who started just like you—with big dreams and a lot of determination. Cole Palmer is not just any football player; he's a shining example of how passion, hard work, and never giving up can lead to amazing achievements!

In this book, you'll discover how Cole's love for football began when he was just a little kid. From playing in his backyard to making it big with Chelsea, Cole's journey is filled with exciting moments, important lessons, and inspiring stories. You'll learn about his family, the friends who helped him along the way, and the challenges he faced on his path to becoming a football star.

So, are you ready to dive into the incredible story of Cole Palmer? Let's explore how this young footballer turned his passion into stardom and see what we can learn from his amazing journey!

Meet Cole Palmer

Who is Cole Palmer?

Cole Palmer is an extraordinary young footballer who has captured the hearts of fans around the world with his incredible skills and dedication. Born on May 6, 2002, in Manchester, England, Cole's journey from a young football enthusiast to a professional player is nothing short of inspiring.

From an early age, Cole showed a remarkable passion for football. With a football in his hands and his family cheering him on, he spent countless hours practicing and dreaming about becoming a star. His father, Jermaine, taught him everything he knew about the game, while his mother, Marie, and older sister, Hallie, provided endless support and encouragement. Cole's journey took him from playing in local clubs to joining Manchester City's youth academy, where his talent truly began to shine. His hard work and determination paid off, leading him to a professional career with Chelsea, where he continues to dazzle fans with his impressive performances. But Cole's story is not just about football. It's about believing in yourself, working hard, and never giving up on your dreams. In the following pages, you'll learn more about Cole's early life, his rise to fame, and the lessons he's learned along the way.

Are you ready to discover the amazing journey of Cole Palmer? Let's get started and explore how this young footballer turned his dreams into reality!

Why Cole Palmer is an Inspiration

What Makes Cole Palmer So Special?

Cole Palmer isn't just a football star; he's an inspiration to kids everywhere. But what makes him so special? Let's explore the qualities that make Cole someone you can look up to and learn from.

1. Passion and Dedication

From a very young age, Cole had a deep love for football. He didn't just play for fun; he practiced hard, dreamed big, and worked tirelessly to improve his skills. His passion for the game drove him to keep going, even when things got tough.

2. Hard Work Pays Off

Cole's journey wasn't always easy. He faced challenges, made sacrifices, and put in countless hours of practice. But his dedication paid off. Cole's story teaches us that hard work and perseverance are key to achieving our goals, no matter how big they may seem.

3. Family Support

Cole's success isn't just about his talent; it's also about the support he received from his family. His father, Jermaine, was his coach and biggest cheerleader, while his mother, Marie, and sister, Hallie, were always there to encourage him. Their support shows how important it is to have people who believe in you.

4. Overcoming Challenges

Every journey has its ups and downs, and Cole's is no exception. He faced setbacks and obstacles along the way, but he didn't let them stop him. Instead, he learned from them and kept pushing forward. Cole's ability to overcome challenges and keep moving towards his dreams is a powerful lesson for us all.

5. Inspiring Others

Cole's story is more than just about football. It's about inspiring others to follow their dreams and believe in themselves. By sharing his journey, Cole shows that with passion, hard work, and determination, anything is possible.

So, why is Cole Palmer an inspiration? Because he proves that dreams can come true with dedication, support, and a never-give-up attitude. His story encourages us to chase our own dreams and believe in our potential.

:

Chapter 1

Growing Up

A Bright Start in Manchester

Cole Palmer was born on May 6, 2002, in the lively city of Manchester, England. From the moment he entered the world, it was clear that he was destined for great things. Manchester is a city known for its rich football history, and little did anyone know, Cole was about to become a part of that legacy.

Family First

Cole grew up in a warm and supportive family. His father, Jermaine, played a huge role in his life, especially when it came to football. Jermaine wasn't just a dad; he was Cole's first coach and mentor. He taught Cole the basics of football and helped him develop his skills from a young age.

His mother, Marie, and older sister, Hallie, were always by his side, cheering him on at every game and supporting his dreams. Hallie, who was born in December 2000, looked up to her younger brother with pride and admiration. The Palmer family was a tight-knit unit, and their love and encouragement were the foundation of Cole's success.

Playing in the Backyard

As a young child, Cole spent countless hours playing football in his backyard. With a makeshift goal and a football at his feet, he practiced dribbling, shooting, and passing. These early practices were more than just fun; they were the beginning of Cole's journey to becoming a football star.

His passion for the game was evident in everything he did. Whether he was playing with friends or practicing on his own, Cole's enthusiasm and determination shone through. It was clear that he had a special talent and a deep love for football.

Early Challenges and Triumphs

Growing up, Cole faced many challenges, like balancing school with football practice and dealing with the ups and downs of youth sports. But with the support of his family and his own strong will, he overcame these obstacles. Each challenge made him stronger and more determined to succeed.

Cole's early experiences were full of learning and growth. He learned the importance of hard work, perseverance, and teamwork. These lessons would become the building blocks of his future success.

A Dream Takes Shape

As Cole grew older, his dream of becoming a football star became clearer. He began playing for local clubs, where his skills and dedication started to stand out. His journey was just beginning, but the foundation had been laid during these formative years in Manchester.

Chapter 1 of Cole Palmer's story is a testament to the power of family support, passion, and hard work. It's where his love for football first took shape and where his journey towards becoming a football star began.

Cole's Early Days in Manchester

A City Full of Energy

Manchester, England, is a vibrant city known for its rich history and love for football. It's a place where football dreams can come true, and it was here that Cole Palmer's journey began. Growing up in this dynamic city, Cole was surrounded by the excitement and passion that Manchester is famous for.

Family and Friends

Cole was born into a close-knit family who loved and supported him every step of the way. His father, Jermaine, was his biggest football fan and coach. Jermaine played an important role in introducing Cole to the game, sharing his knowledge, and helping him develop his skills.

Cole's mother, Marie, was always there to encourage him, whether he was practicing in the backyard or playing in a local match. His older sister, Hallie, also played a big part in his life. Born in December 2000, Hallie was both a role model and a cheerleader for her younger brother. The Palmer family's unwavering support gave Cole the confidence to chase his dreams.

A Backyard Football Star

In the early days, Cole could often be found in his family's backyard, where he spent hours playing football. With a makeshift goal and a football at his feet, he practiced dribbling, shooting, and scoring goals. These backyard sessions were more than just playtime—they were the first steps towards Cole's future as a footballer.

His dedication was evident from a young age. Even though he was just a child, Cole's love for football was palpable. He would often imagine himself playing in grand stadiums and scoring winning goals, and he worked hard to turn those dreams into reality.

School and Local Football

As Cole grew older, he balanced his school life with his growing passion for football. He joined local football teams where he began to make a name for himself. His talent and enthusiasm were noticeable, and he quickly became a standout player in his local community.

The support from his family, combined with his own determination, helped Cole excel in both school and football. His early days in Manchester were marked by hard work, support, and a strong desire to succeed. These formative years laid the groundwork for the incredible journey that lay ahead.

The Beginning of a Dream

Cole's early experiences in Manchester were filled with learning and growing. His love for football was nurtured by his family and friends, and his skills began to shine. It was in these early days that Cole's dream of becoming a football star started to take shape.

As he continued to play and develop his skills, it became clear that Cole Palmer was on a path to something special. The city of Manchester, with its rich football heritage and supportive community, was the perfect backdrop for his journey to greatness.

Family and Friends Who Supported Him

A Strong Family Foundation

Cole Palmer's journey to becoming a football star was built on a solid foundation of love and support from his family. His father, Jermaine, played a crucial role in Cole's early development as a footballer. Jermaine wasn't just a dad; he was a coach, mentor, and biggest fan. He spent countless hours teaching Cole the fundamentals of football, sharing his own experiences, and encouraging Cole to pursue his passion.

Cole's mother, Marie, provided endless encouragement and support. She was always there to cheer him on during matches and practices, offering a comforting presence and words of motivation. Marie's belief in Cole's abilities helped him stay confident and focused, even when faced with challenges.

A Sister's Pride

Cole's older sister, Hallie, born in December 2000, was another important figure in his life. As his big sister, Hallie was both a role model and a source of inspiration. She took pride in Cole's achievements and was always there to celebrate his successes. Whether it was a big win or a small victory, Hallie's pride in her younger brother was unwavering.

Friends on the Field

In addition to his family, Cole was fortunate to have a group of friends who shared his love for football. These friends played a significant role in his development, both on and off the field. Together, they spent countless hours practicing, playing, and pushing each other to improve. Their camaraderie and friendly competition helped Cole hone his skills and develop a deeper understanding of the game.

Community Support

Growing up in Manchester, Cole was part of a community that valued football and celebrated its players. Local coaches, teammates, and community members recognized Cole's talent and potential early on. They provided guidance, opportunities, and encouragement, helping him navigate the challenges of youth football and paving the way for his future success.

Believing in Dreams

The support from Cole's family and friends was more than just cheering from the sidelines; it was a constant reminder that he was not alone in his journey. Their belief in his dreams and their willingness to invest time and effort into his development made a significant difference. With a strong support system behind him, Cole was able to face obstacles with resilience and pursue his goals with determination.

A Team Effort

Cole Palmer's story is a testament to the power of family and community. It highlights how the collective support of loved ones can inspire and propel someone towards greatness. From his parents' dedication to his sister's pride and the encouragement of friends and coaches, every bit of support played a role in shaping Cole's path to becoming a football star.

As we continue to follow Cole's journey, we'll see how this strong foundation of support helped him rise through the ranks and achieve his dreams. His story reminds us that while individual talent is important, the love and encouragement of family and friends are what truly make dreams possible.

Chapter 2

Discovering Football

A Newfound Love for the Game

Cole Palmer's journey into the world of football began at a very young age. Growing up in Manchester, a city renowned for its football culture, Cole was naturally drawn to the sport. His first exposure to football came through watching games on TV with his family, where he was mesmerized by the skill and excitement of the professional players.

Playing in the Backyard

One of Cole's earliest memories of football is playing in the backyard with his father, Jermaine. They would spend hours kicking the ball around, practicing dribbling, and pretending to be famous footballers. Jermaine's love for the game was contagious, and he shared his knowledge and passion with young Cole, teaching him the basics and encouraging him to have fun.

First Football Experiences

Cole's first organized football experience came when he joined a local youth team. He was just a small kid with big dreams, but his enthusiasm and talent quickly stood out. Playing with other children his age, Cole discovered the joy of teamwork, the thrill of competition, and the importance of practice.

Early Training and Skills

Even at a young age, Cole was dedicated to improving his skills. He spent countless hours practicing dribbling, passing, and shooting. His backyard became his training ground, where he would try to mimic the moves of his football idols. With each practice session, his confidence grew, and his love for the game deepened.

Encouragement from Coaches

Cole was fortunate to have supportive coaches who recognized his potential. They provided guidance and encouragement, helping him develop his abilities and understand the game better. These early coaches played a crucial role in shaping Cole's football journey, offering valuable lessons that would stay with him throughout his career.

The Joy of Playing

For Cole, football was more than just a sport; it was a source of happiness and excitement. He loved the feeling of scoring a goal, the camaraderie with his teammates, and the thrill of a well-played match. Football brought joy into his life, and he couldn't imagine doing anything else.

The First Big Break

Cole's dedication and hard work paid off when he got the opportunity to join Manchester City's youth academy. This was a dream come true for the young footballer, and it marked the beginning of a new chapter in his life. At the academy, he received top-notch training and competed against some of the best young talents in the country.

A Future in Football

As Cole continued to develop his skills and grow as a player, his passion for football only intensified. He knew that he wanted to pursue a career in the sport and was willing to put in the effort to make that dream a reality. With the support of his family, coaches, and teammates, Cole was ready to take on the challenges ahead and work towards becoming a professional footballer.

Looking Ahead

Cole Palmer's discovery of football was just the start of an incredible journey. His early experiences, the support he received, and his unwavering passion for the game laid the groundwork for his future success. In the next chapters, we'll explore how Cole's talent and determination led him to rise through the ranks and achieve his dreams of playing at the highest level.

How Cole Fell in Love with Football

A Spark of Passion

Cole Palmer's love for football began as a spark that quickly turned into a blazing passion. Growing up in Manchester, a city with a deep football heritage, Cole was surrounded by the sport from a very young age. His earliest memories include watching matches on TV with his family and feeling the excitement of the game.

Inspiration from Football Legends

Watching legendary football players on TV left a significant impact on Cole. He admired their skills, dedication, and the way they played with such joy and passion. This inspired him to dream of becoming a footballer himself. He often imagined himself scoring goals in big stadiums, just like his idols.

A Football Gift

One day, Cole received a football as a gift from his father, Jermaine. With his new football, Cole spent hours practicing in his backyard, trying to replicate the moves he had seen on TV. This was the beginning of his journey into the world of football.

Playing with Family and Friends

Backyard Adventures

The Palmer family's backyard was where Cole's football journey truly began. With his father, Jermaine, as his first coach, Cole learned the basics of dribbling, passing, and shooting. Jermaine's love for football was evident in the way he taught and encouraged Cole, making each practice session fun and exciting.

Friendly Matches

Cole often played football with his older sister, Hallie, and his friends from the neighborhood. These friendly matches were filled with laughter, competition, and a lot of learning. Playing with Hallie, who was born in December 2000, added a special bond to their sibling relationship. Hallie's pride in her younger brother's skills was clear, and she always supported him.

Neighborhood Heroes

The neighborhood kids quickly recognized Cole's talent and enthusiasm for the game. They looked up to him and enjoyed playing together, whether it was a casual kickabout or a more organized match. These early games helped Cole develop not only his football skills but also important life skills like teamwork, sportsmanship, and leadership.

Local Football Clubs

Cole's passion for football led him to join local football clubs where he could play more competitively. These clubs provided him with structured training and the opportunity to compete against other young players. The support from his coaches and teammates further fueled his love for the game and helped him improve his skills.

A Supportive Community

The local community played a significant role in Cole's early football experiences. Coaches, neighbors, and family friends all recognized his potential and cheered him on. Their encouragement and belief in his abilities gave Cole the confidence to pursue his dreams.

Building Dreams

Playing with family and friends laid the foundation for Cole's football journey. These early experiences were filled with joy, learning, and growth. They shaped his character and fueled his determination to become a professional footballer. The support and love from his family and friends were crucial in helping him take the first steps towards his dream.

Chapter 3

Starting Young

A Budding Talent

Cole Palmer's love for football was evident from the start, and it wasn't long before his parents realized that their son had a special talent for the game. His early backyard practices, along with playing with friends and family, had prepared him for something more structured. At a young age, Cole took his first steps into organized football, where his skills would be put to the test and his passion for the game would grow even stronger.

Joining Local Football Clubs

Finding His First Team

Cole's journey into organized football began when he joined his first local football club. This was a significant milestone in his young life. The club provided a platform for Cole to develop his skills in a more formal setting, surrounded by other young players who shared his love for the game.

Joining the club was an exciting moment for Cole. It was a place where he could meet new friends, learn from experienced coaches, and play football at a higher level. His enthusiasm was matched by his determination to improve with each training session and match.

Learning the Ropes

At the local club, Cole was introduced to the fundamentals of the game in a more structured way. He learned the importance of teamwork, strategy, and discipline. The drills and exercises were more challenging than the backyard games, but Cole embraced them eagerly. He was like a sponge, absorbing everything his coaches taught him.

Cole's coaches quickly noticed his potential. His natural talent, combined with his work ethic and eagerness to learn, set him apart from many of his peers. The club became a second home for Cole, a place where he could immerse himself in football and dream of one day playing professionally.

Building Friendships

The club was also where Cole formed lasting friendships with his teammates. These were kids who, like him, loved football and were excited to play and learn together. The camaraderie among the players made the practices and matches even more enjoyable. They celebrated victories together and supported each other through tough times.

The Fun and Challenges of Youth Football

The Joy of the Game

For Cole, playing football was always fun. Whether it was scoring a goal, making a perfect pass, or simply being on the pitch, he loved every moment of it. Youth football was a time of discovery and joy, where the focus was on playing the game he loved without the pressures that would come later in his career.

Cole thrived on the excitement of match days. The thrill of putting on his kit, stepping onto the field, and hearing the cheers from the sidelines was something he looked forward to every week. The smiles, high-fives, and team spirit made every game memorable.

Facing Challenges

But youth football wasn't without its challenges. As Cole progressed, the competition became tougher. He faced stronger opponents, and the expectations from coaches and teammates grew. There were times when things didn't go as planned—matches were lost, mistakes were made, and frustrations arose.

However, these challenges were also opportunities for growth. Cole learned to handle pressure, deal with setbacks, and stay focused on his goals. His parents, coaches, and teammates provided the support he needed to keep going, reminding him that every challenge was a chance to learn and improve.

Balancing School and Football

Another challenge for Cole was balancing his love for football with his responsibilities at school. Like many young athletes, he had to manage his time carefully, making sure he kept up with his studies while still dedicating enough time to practice and matches. It wasn't always easy, but Cole's passion for football gave him the motivation to work hard in both areas.

Developing a Strong Work Ethic

Through the fun and challenges of youth football, Cole developed a strong work ethic. He understood that talent alone wasn't enough to succeed; it took hard work, dedication, and a willingness to push through difficult times. These lessons were invaluable as he continued his journey towards becoming a professional footballer.

Chapter 4

Rising Through the Ranks

A Young Star in the Making

As Cole Palmer continued to impress with his talent and dedication, his football journey took a significant step forward. His hard work at the local football clubs did not go unnoticed, and soon, he was presented with an incredible opportunity that would bring him closer to his dream of becoming a professional footballer.

Moving Up to Manchester City's Academy

A Dream Come True

One of the most exciting moments in Cole's young life was when he was invited to join Manchester City's Academy. Manchester City is one of the top football clubs in the world, and their academy is known for developing young talents into professional stars. For Cole, this was a dream come true.

Intense Training and Development

Joining Manchester City's Academy meant more rigorous training and higher expectations. The coaches at the academy were experienced and knowledgeable, pushing Cole to reach new heights. The training sessions were intense, focusing on every aspect of the game—from technical skills to tactical understanding.

Cole's days were filled with drills, exercises, and matches designed to hone his abilities. The competition was fierce, with many talented young players vying for a spot in the senior team. But Cole was determined to stand out. He embraced the challenge, knowing that this was a crucial step in his journey.

Learning from the Best

At Manchester City's Academy, Cole had the opportunity to learn from some of the best coaches and former players. Their guidance and mentorship were invaluable. They taught him not just about the game, but also about the importance of discipline, teamwork, and professionalism. The academy also provided state-of-the-art facilities, giving Cole access to top-notch resources to aid his development. It was an environment where he could thrive and grow, both as a player and as a person.

Important Moments in Cole's Youth Career

First Academy Match

One of the most memorable moments for Cole at the academy was his first match. Wearing the Manchester City kit and stepping onto the pitch was a surreal experience. He was nervous but excited, ready to show what he could do. Cole played with determination and skill, earning praise from his coaches and teammates.

Overcoming Challenges

There were times when things didn't go as smoothly. Cole faced tough opponents, experienced losses, and dealt with the pressures of high expectations. But each challenge was a learning opportunity. He worked harder, listened to his coaches, and kept pushing forward. These experiences made him stronger and more resilient.

Winning Tournaments

Cole's efforts paid off when he helped his team win several youth tournaments. These victories were a testament to his growth as a player and his ability to perform under pressure. The joy of lifting a trophy with his teammates was indescribable and fueled his desire to achieve even more.

Scoring Memorable Goals

Throughout his time at the academy, Cole scored many memorable goals. Each goal was a result of his hard work and determination. Whether it was a stunning long-range shot or a skillful dribble past defenders, these moments showcased his talent and potential.

Recognition and Awards

Cole's performances didn't go unnoticed. He received various awards and accolades, recognizing his contributions to the team and his development as a player. These recognitions were a source of pride for Cole and his family, motivating him to keep striving for excellence.

Support from Family and Friends

Throughout his journey, Cole's family and friends remained his biggest supporters. They attended his matches, cheered him on, and provided unwavering support. Their belief in him was a constant source of strength, helping him stay focused and motivated.

Looking Ahead

Cole Palmer's time at Manchester City's Academy was filled with important moments that shaped his youth career. It was a period of growth, learning, and achievement. With each milestone, Cole moved closer to his dream of becoming a professional footballer. As he continued to rise through the ranks, the future looked bright for this young star.

Chapter 5

Making It Professional

A Dream Realized

After years of hard work, dedication, and countless hours on the training pitch, Cole Palmer's dream of becoming a professional footballer was finally within reach. His talent, perseverance, and passion for the game had brought him to this pivotal moment in his career.

Cole's Big Break with Chelsea

A Life-Changing Opportunity

Cole Palmer's big break came when he was signed by Chelsea, one of the most prestigious football clubs in the world. Moving from Manchester City's Academy to Chelsea was a significant step in his career. It was a chance to showcase his abilities on a much larger stage and compete at the highest level of the sport.

Joining Chelsea

Signing with Chelsea was a thrilling experience for Cole. He was welcomed by his new teammates and coaches, who were excited to have such a promising young talent join their ranks. The transition to a new club came with its challenges, but Cole was ready to embrace them. He knew that this was the opportunity he had been working towards his entire life.

First Impressions

Cole quickly made a positive impression at Chelsea. His work ethic, skill, and determination stood out during training sessions. He was eager to learn from his new coaches and experienced teammates, absorbing as much knowledge as he could. Cole's attitude and dedication earned him respect within the team and set the stage for his professional debut.

His First Big Games and Achievements

Making His Professional Debut

Cole Palmer's professional debut for Chelsea was a moment he would never forget. Stepping onto the pitch in front of thousands of cheering fans, wearing the iconic blue jersey, was a dream come true. The nerves were there, but so was the excitement and determination to prove himself.

Memorable Performances

In his first few games, Cole showcased his talent and potential. His performances were marked by quick dribbling, precise passing, and a keen eye for goal. He played with confidence and flair, earning praise from fans, teammates, and coaches alike. Each match was an opportunity to learn and improve, and Cole seized every moment.

Scoring His First Goal

One of the highlights of Cole's early professional career was scoring his first goal for Chelsea. The goal came in a crucial match, and it was a moment of pure joy and celebration. His teammates rushed to congratulate him, and the fans erupted in applause. This goal was a testament to his hard work and a sign of more great things to come.

Key Achievements

As Cole continued to play, he began to achieve significant milestones in his career. He contributed to important victories, helped Chelsea secure crucial points in the league, and played a key role in cup competitions. His consistent performances and ability to rise to the occasion in big matches quickly established him as an important player for the team.

Winning Trophies

Cole's efforts were rewarded when Chelsea won major trophies. Being part of a title-winning team was a dream come true. Lifting the trophy with his teammates was a proud moment, symbolizing the culmination of years of hard work and dedication. These victories were not just personal achievements but also highlights in Chelsea's illustrious history.

Recognition and Praise

Cole's impact on the pitch did not go unnoticed. He received accolades and recognition from football pundits, former players, and fans. His name began to appear in discussions about the best young talents in football. The praise and recognition were affirmations of his abilities and potential to become a star in the sport.

Support System

Throughout his journey, Cole's family remained his biggest supporters. His parents, Jermaine and Marie, and his sister Hallie were there for every milestone, cheering him on and celebrating his successes. Their unwavering support gave Cole the strength to overcome challenges and continue striving for greatness.

Looking Forward

Cole Palmer's early professional career with Chelsea was marked by memorable moments, significant achievements, and personal growth. But this was just the beginning. With each game, he aimed to improve, learn, and contribute to his team's success. The future held endless possibilities for this young football star, and he was ready to seize every opportunity.

Chapter 6

Facing Challenges

Every Journey Has Its Hurdles

As Cole Palmer's career progressed, he encountered various challenges that tested his resolve and determination. The path to success is never easy, and Cole had to learn to overcome obstacles and stay motivated through tough times. This chapter highlights his resilience and the lessons he learned along the way.

Overcoming Obstacles on the Road to Success

Injuries and Setbacks

One of the biggest challenges Cole faced was dealing with injuries. Like many athletes, he experienced times when injuries kept him off the pitch. These moments were tough for Cole, as they disrupted his progress and made it difficult to maintain his form. However, he learned the importance of patience and proper recovery.

During his recovery periods, Cole focused on staying positive and doing everything he could to come back stronger. He followed the advice of medical professionals, worked hard on his rehabilitation exercises, and maintained a healthy lifestyle. His dedication paid off, and he returned to the field with renewed energy and determination.

Competition for Spots

As a young player in a top club like Chelsea, Cole faced intense competition for a place in the starting lineup. The team was filled with talented players, each eager to prove themselves. This competition was a double-edged sword; it pushed Cole to improve but also presented a constant challenge to secure his spot.

Cole embraced this challenge by giving his best in every training session and match. He knew that consistent hard work and impressive performances were key to earning his place. The competition made him a better player and taught him the value of perseverance and resilience.

Balancing Football and Personal Life

Balancing the demands of a professional football career with personal life was another challenge Cole had to navigate. The rigorous training schedules, travel for matches, and media attention could be overwhelming. It was important for Cole to find time for himself, his family, and his friends.

He managed this balance by staying organized and prioritizing his time. Cole made sure to spend quality time with his family, who were his biggest supporters. Their love and encouragement helped him stay grounded and focused on his goals.

Handling Pressure and Expectations

As Cole's profile grew, so did the pressure and expectations. Fans, coaches, and the media had high hopes for his performances. The weight of these expectations could be daunting, but Cole learned to handle it with grace.

He focused on what he could control—his effort, attitude, and preparation. By staying dedicated to his training and trusting in his abilities, Cole was able to manage the pressure and deliver strong performances. He also learned the importance of mental toughness and maintaining a positive mindset.

Staying Positive and Motivated

Setting Goals

One of the ways Cole stayed motivated was by setting clear goals for himself. These goals ranged from short-term objectives, like improving specific skills, to long-term aspirations, like winning major trophies. Having goals gave him a sense of direction and purpose, motivating him to keep pushing forward.

Finding Inspiration

Cole found inspiration in various sources. He looked up to football legends who had overcome their own challenges to achieve greatness. Their stories served as reminders that perseverance and hard work could lead to success. Cole also drew inspiration from his teammates, coaches, and the support of his fans.

Maintaining a Support Network

A strong support network was crucial for Cole's motivation. His family, friends, and coaches provided unwavering support and encouragement. They celebrated his successes and helped him through tough times. Knowing that he had a team of people who believed in him kept Cole motivated and focused.

Learning from Setbacks

Instead of being discouraged by setbacks, Cole viewed them as learning opportunities. Each challenge he faced taught him valuable lessons and helped him grow as a player and person. This mindset allowed him to turn obstacles into stepping stones on his path to success.

Staying Passionate

Above all, Cole's love for football kept him motivated. His passion for the game was the driving force behind everything he did. No matter how tough things got, his enthusiasm for playing football never waned. This passion fueled his dedication and commitment to achieving his dreams.

Cole Palmer's journey was filled with challenges, but his ability to overcome them was a testament to his resilience and determination. By staying positive, setting goals, and maintaining a strong support network, Cole was able to navigate the ups and downs of his career. His story is an inspiration to young footballers everywhere, showing that with hard work and perseverance, anything is possible.

Chapter 7

Life Outside Football

Beyond the Pitch

While football is a major part of Cole Palmer's life, there is more to him than just being a talented athlete. This chapter explores the aspects of Cole's life outside of football, including his hobbies, interests, and involvement with his family and community. It provides a glimpse into the person behind the player.

Hobbies and Interests

A Love for Music

When Cole is not on the football field, one of his favorite activities is listening to music. He enjoys a variety of genres, from upbeat pop tunes to relaxing classical melodies. Music helps him unwind after a long day of training and matches. It's a way for him to relax and recharge.

Playing Video Games

Like many young people, Cole loves playing video games. It's a fun way for him to spend his free time and connect with friends. Whether he's competing in a virtual football match or exploring new worlds in adventure games, Cole finds video games to be a great way to unwind and have fun.

Enjoying Nature

Cole also has a love for the outdoors. He enjoys spending time in nature, whether it's going for a hike, having a picnic in the park, or simply taking a walk. Being outside helps him clear his mind and appreciate the beauty of the natural world. It's a peaceful escape from the fast-paced life of professional football.

Reading and Learning

Cole is always eager to learn new things. He enjoys reading books on various topics, from history to science fiction. Reading not only entertains him but also broadens his knowledge and perspective. Cole believes that staying curious and informed is important for personal growth.

Fitness and Wellness

Maintaining his fitness is crucial for Cole, but he also enjoys exploring different wellness activities. Whether it's practicing yoga for flexibility and relaxation or trying out new healthy recipes, Cole is dedicated to taking care of his body and mind. He understands the importance of a balanced lifestyle for overall well-being.

Cole's Family and Community Involvement

Family Time

Family is incredibly important to Cole. He cherishes the moments he spends with his parents, Jermaine and Marie, and his older sister, Hallie. Despite his busy schedule, Cole makes sure to prioritize family time. They enjoy simple activities like family dinners, watching movies, and celebrating special occasions together.

Giving Back to the Community

Cole believes in the importance of giving back to the community that has supported him throughout his journey. He is involved in various charitable activities and community projects. Whether it's visiting local schools to inspire young kids or participating in charity football matches, Cole is dedicated to making a positive impact.

Supporting Local Initiatives

In addition to his charitable work, Cole supports local initiatives that promote sports and education. He understands the value of providing opportunities for young people to pursue their passions, just as he was given the chance to follow his football dreams. Cole's involvement in these initiatives reflects his commitment to helping others achieve their potential.

Role Model and Mentor

As a successful young footballer, Cole takes his role as a mentor seriously. He often visits youth football academies and clubs to share his experiences and offer advice to aspiring players. He emphasizes the importance of hard work, dedication, and believing in oneself. Cole's guidance and encouragement inspire many young athletes to pursue their dreams.

Staying Humble and Grounded

Despite his success, Cole remains humble and grounded. He never forgets the support and love from his family and community that helped him get to where he is today. Cole's humility and gratitude are evident in the way he interacts with fans, teammates, and everyone he meets.

Cole Palmer's life outside of football is filled with activities and interests that bring him joy and fulfillment. From his hobbies and personal pursuits to his dedication to family and community, Cole is a well-rounded individual who values the things that matter most. His story is not just about football but also about the importance of staying true to oneself and giving back to others.

Chapter 8

Cole's Football Journey

The Path of a Rising Star

Cole Palmer's journey through the world of football has been filled with unforgettable moments and valuable lessons. This chapter delves into some of the most memorable matches and highlights of his career, as well as the important lessons he has learned from playing the beautiful game.

Memorable Matches and Highlights

The First Goal

One of the most memorable moments in Cole's career was scoring his first goal for Chelsea. It was a thrilling match, and the excitement of seeing the ball hit the back of the net was indescribable. His teammates celebrated with him, and the fans cheered loudly. This goal marked the beginning of many more incredible achievements.

UEFA Youth League Triumph

During his time with Manchester City's Academy, Cole played a pivotal role in the team's victory in the UEFA Youth League. His performances throughout the tournament were outstanding, showcasing his skill and determination. Winning the prestigious youth competition was a significant milestone and a testament to Cole's talent.

Premier League Debut

Cole's debut in the Premier League was a dream come true. Playing in one of the most competitive leagues in the world was a huge step in his career. The match was intense, but Cole's composure and skill shone through. His debut performance earned praise from fans and pundits alike, solidifying his place in the team.

National Team Call-Up

Another highlight of Cole's career was being called up to represent England at the youth level. Wearing the national team jersey and playing alongside some of the country's best young talents was an honor. Cole's performances on the international stage were impressive, and he proudly represented his country in various tournaments.

Key Matches for Chelsea

Throughout his time with Chelsea, Cole has been involved in several key matches that showcased his abilities. Whether it was scoring crucial goals, providing assists, or making important defensive plays, Cole consistently proved his worth on the field. His contributions have helped Chelsea secure vital wins and compete for top honors.

Memorable Champions League Nights

Playing in the UEFA Champions League is a dream for any footballer, and Cole had the opportunity to do so with Chelsea. The electrifying atmosphere, the high level of competition, and the chance to face some of the best teams in Europe made these matches unforgettable. Cole's performances in the Champions League were remarkable, and he gained invaluable experience from playing on such a grand stage.

Lessons Learned from Playing Football

The Value of Hard Work

One of the most important lessons Cole learned from football is the value of hard work. Success on the pitch requires dedication, discipline, and relentless effort. Cole's journey taught him that there are no shortcuts to achieving greatness. Every training session, every match, and every moment of practice contributed to his growth as a player.

Teamwork and Collaboration

Football is a team sport, and Cole learned the significance of teamwork and collaboration. Working together with his teammates, understanding each other's strengths and weaknesses, and supporting one another were crucial elements of success. Cole realized that achieving goals requires collective effort and that every player has a vital role to play.

Resilience in the Face of Adversity

Throughout his career, Cole faced numerous challenges and setbacks. Injuries, tough matches, and moments of doubt tested his resilience. However, he learned to stay strong and keep pushing forward. Overcoming adversity taught Cole the importance of perseverance and believing in oneself, even when the going gets tough.

The Importance of Sportsmanship

Cole always valued the importance of sportsmanship, both on and off the field. Respecting opponents, playing fair, and maintaining a positive attitude were essential principles he followed. Cole understood that football is not just about winning but also about showing respect and integrity.

Learning from Failure

Failure is a part of any journey, and Cole experienced his fair share of disappointments. However, he learned to view failure as an opportunity for growth. Each setback provided valuable lessons and motivated him to work harder. Cole's ability to learn from his mistakes and come back stronger was a key factor in his success.

The Joy of Playing Football

Above all, Cole's football journey reminded him of the joy and passion he has for the game. Despite the pressures and challenges, his love for football remained unwavering. Playing the sport he loves, experiencing the thrill of competition, and connecting with fans were the driving forces behind his dedication.

Cole Palmer's football journey has been a remarkable adventure filled with memorable matches, important lessons, and personal growth. From his early days in Manchester to making his mark at Chelsea, Cole's story is a testament to the power of hard work, resilience, and passion. His journey continues to inspire young footballers around the world, showing that with determination and a love for the game, dreams can come true.

Chapter 9

Advice for Young Dreamers

Inspiring the Next Generation

Cole Palmer's journey from a young boy with a passion for football to a professional player at Chelsea is a source of inspiration for many aspiring footballers. In this chapter, Cole shares his advice for young dreamers who want to follow in his footsteps. His tips and insights highlight the importance of hard work, dedication, and a love for the game.

Tips from Cole Palmer for Kids Who Want to Play Football

1. Follow Your Passion

"The most important thing is to love what you do," says Cole. "If you have a passion for football, let that drive you. Enjoy every moment on the pitch and never lose sight of why you started playing in the first place."

2. Practice Regularly

"Practice makes perfect," Cole emphasizes. "Spend time honing your skills, whether it's dribbling, passing, shooting, or defending. The more you practice, the better you'll become. Don't be afraid to put in the extra hours."

3. Listen to Your Coaches

"Coaches are there to help you improve," Cole advises. "Listen to their feedback and learn from their experience. They can provide valuable insights that will help you develop your game."

4. Stay Fit and Healthy

"Football requires a lot of physical fitness," Cole reminds young players. "Eat a balanced diet, stay hydrated, and get plenty of rest. Taking care of your body is essential for performing well on the pitch."

5. Be a Team Player

"Remember, football is a team sport," Cole says. "Work with your teammates, support each other, and communicate well on the field. Success comes from working together and understanding each other's strengths."

6. Keep a Positive Attitude

"There will be ups and downs, but it's important to stay positive," Cole encourages. "Learn from your mistakes and use them as opportunities to grow. A positive attitude will help you overcome challenges and stay motivated."

7. Set Goals and Work Towards Them

"Set both short-term and long-term goals," Cole suggests. "Having goals gives you something to strive for and keeps you focused. Whether it's improving a particular skill or making it to a higher-level team, work hard to achieve your objectives."

8. Have Fun

"Most importantly, have fun," Cole concludes. "Football is a beautiful game, and it should bring you joy. Enjoy playing, learning, and growing as a footballer."

The Importance of Hard Work and Dedication

Consistency is Key

Cole's journey to becoming a professional footballer was not an overnight success. It required consistent effort and dedication over many years. He stresses the importance of being consistent in your training and giving your best effort every day.

Embrace the Grind

"Football isn't always easy," Cole admits. "There are early mornings, tough training sessions, and sacrifices you have to make. Embrace the grind and understand that these efforts are necessary to reach your goals."

Learn from Every Experience

"Every match, whether you win or lose, is a learning experience," Cole says. "Reflect on your performances, understand what you did well and where you can improve. Each game is an opportunity to grow."

Stay Motivated

"Find what motivates you and use it to fuel your journey," Cole advises. "Whether it's the dream of playing in a big stadium, the support of your family, or the desire to be the best, keep that motivation alive."

Persevere Through Challenges

"There will be tough times, but don't give up," Cole encourages. "Perseverance is key to overcoming obstacles. Stay focused on your dreams and keep pushing forward, no matter what challenges you face."

Believe in Yourself

"Believe in your abilities and have confidence in yourself," Cole emphasizes. "Self-belief is crucial for success. Trust that your hard work will pay off and that you have what it takes to achieve your dreams."

Cole Palmer's advice for young dreamers highlights the importance of passion, practice, and perseverance. By following his tips and maintaining a strong work ethic, aspiring footballers can pursue their dreams and strive for greatness. Cole's journey serves as a reminder that with dedication and a love for the game, anything is possible.

CONCLUSION

A Journey of Inspiration

Cole Palmer's story is one of determination, hard work, and passion. From his early days in Manchester to achieving success as a professional footballer with Chelsea, Cole's journey serves as an inspiring example for young dreamers everywhere. This conclusion reflects on the key lessons from Cole's life and offers encouragement to kids who aspire to follow their own dreams.

What We Can Learn from Cole Palmer's Story

The Power of Passion

Cole Palmer's love for football was the driving force behind his success. His story teaches us that having a passion for something is essential. When you truly love what you do, it fuels your motivation and helps you overcome challenges. Cole's dedication to football shows that following your passion can lead to incredible achievements.

The Importance of Hard Work

Cole's journey highlights that success doesn't come easily. It requires hard work, practice, and perseverance. Whether it's practicing on the field, listening to coaches, or staying fit, Cole's commitment to putting in the effort is a powerful reminder that hard work is key to reaching your goals.

Learning from Challenges

Every successful person faces obstacles along the way, and Cole is no exception. His ability to learn from challenges and setbacks demonstrates that difficulties are opportunities for growth. By facing challenges with resilience and a positive attitude, you can turn obstacles into stepping stones toward success.

The Value of Teamwork

Football is a team sport, and Cole's experiences emphasize the importance of working well with others. Teamwork, communication, and supporting your teammates are crucial aspects of success. Cole's story teaches us that collaborating with others and valuing their contributions can lead to greater achievements.

The Joy of the Journey

Throughout his career, Cole has shown that enjoying the journey is as important as reaching the destination. His love for football and the joy he finds in playing and learning remind us that pursuing our dreams should be a fulfilling and enjoyable experience.

Encouragement for Kids to Follow Their Dreams

Believe in Yourself

The most important message from Cole Palmer's story is to believe in yourself. No matter how big or small your dreams may seem, self-belief is crucial. Trust in your abilities, stay focused on your goals, and know that you have the potential to achieve great things.

Stay Dedicated

Dedication and commitment are essential for turning dreams into reality. Keep working hard, practicing regularly, and putting in the effort. Remember that every step you take, no matter how small, brings you closer to your goals.

Embrace the Journey

Enjoy the process of pursuing your dreams. Embrace the highs and lows, the victories and setbacks. The journey itself is a valuable part of achieving your dreams and will help you grow and learn along the way.

Never Give Up

There will be times when things are challenging, and you may feel like giving up. But don't let setbacks stop you. Perseverance is key. Keep pushing forward, stay motivated, and continue working toward your goals.

Seek Support

Don't be afraid to seek support from family, friends, and mentors. They can offer encouragement, advice, and guidance. Surround yourself with people who believe in you and your dreams.

Have Fun

Lastly, remember to have fun. Whether you're playing football or pursuing any other passion, enjoy the experience. Passion and joy will keep you motivated and make the journey enjoyable.

Final Thoughts

Cole Palmer's story is a testament to the power of dreams, hard work, and perseverance. As you follow your own dreams, take inspiration from Cole's journey and remember that with passion, dedication, and a positive attitude, you too can achieve great things. Keep dreaming, keep striving, and never stop believing in yourself.

Fun Facts About Cole Palmer

Discovering More About Cole

Cole Palmer is not just a talented footballer; he's also a person with unique interests and intriguing quirks. Here are some fun facts and interesting tidbits about Cole that you might not know!

Interesting Tidbits and Trivia

1. A Young Prodigy

Cole Palmer joined Manchester City's Academy at a very young age and quickly made a name for himself. His exceptional skills and dedication to the sport were evident from an early age, and he was often regarded as a football prodigy.

2. Multi-Talented

In addition to his football skills, Cole is known for his versatility. He's comfortable playing in various positions on the field, whether it's as a winger, attacking midfielder, or even as a forward. His adaptability makes him a valuable asset to his team.

3. Football Family

Football runs in Cole's family. His father, Jermaine, played a significant role in teaching Cole the fundamentals of the game. Cole often credits his family, especially his dad, for their support and guidance throughout his football journey.

4. A Fan of Music

When he's not on the pitch, Cole enjoys listening to music. He has a diverse taste in music and loves exploring different genres. Music helps him relax and unwind after intense training sessions and matches.

5. A Competitive Spirit

Cole's competitive nature isn't limited to football. He enjoys playing video games and often competes with friends and teammates. His love for gaming reflects his desire to always challenge himself and have fun.

6. An Avid Reader

Cole has a keen interest in reading. He enjoys books on various subjects, including fiction, history, and sports biographies. Reading is one of his favorite ways to relax and gain new perspectives.

7. A Champion in the Making

Cole Palmer was part of the Manchester City squad that won the UEFA Youth League. His contributions were instrumental in the team's success, showcasing his talent and potential at a young age.

8. Fashion Enthusiast

Cole has a great sense of style and enjoys expressing himself through fashion. He often shares his fashion choices and style inspirations on social media, where fans can see his unique and trendy outfits.

9. A Charity Supporter

Cole is passionate about giving back to the community. He participates in various charity events and supports causes that are important to him. His involvement in charitable activities reflects his commitment to making a positive impact.

10. A Role Model

Cole Palmer is a role model for many young footballers. His dedication, hard work, and achievements inspire aspiring athletes to follow their dreams and strive for success, just as he has.

Cole Palmer's life is filled with fascinating details and fun facts that add to his charm and appeal. From his football achievements to his personal interests and passions, Cole's story is a blend of talent, personality, and inspiration. These fun facts offer a glimpse into the world of a young football star who continues to make a mark on and off the pitch.

GLOSSARY

Simple Definitions of Football Terms

Football can be full of unique terms and jargon that might be new to young readers. This glossary provides simple definitions to help you understand some common football terms and concepts.

Assist
A pass or play made by a player that directly helps a teammate score a goal.

Attacker
A player who is primarily responsible for trying to score goals and create offensive plays.

Back Heel
A technique where a player uses the back of their heel to pass or redirect the ball.

Defender
A player who focuses on stopping the opposing team from scoring goals and protecting their own goal.

Dribble
The skill of controlling and moving the ball with short, quick touches while running or walking.

Forward
An attacking player who plays closer to the opponent's goal and aims to score.

Goalkeeper
The player who guards the goal and tries to stop the ball from entering the net. Also known as a goalie.

Header
Using the head to strike or redirect the ball, often used for scoring or passing.

Midfielder
A player who plays in the middle of the field and helps both in attacking and defending.

Penalty Kick
A free kick taken from a spot 12 yards from the goal, awarded for a foul committed inside the penalty area.

Pitch
The field where football is played. Also known as the playing surface or soccer field.

Referee
The official who oversees the match, enforces the

rules, and makes decisions on fouls and other incidents.

Substitute
A player who comes off the bench to replace a teammate during the game.

Tackle
The action of trying to take the ball away from an opponent by using one's feet or body.

Throw-In
The method of restarting play when the ball goes out of bounds over the sideline. The player throws the ball in with both hands from behind their head.

Wing
The areas on the sides of the pitch where players often make crosses and runs.

Yellow Card
A warning given to a player for a foul or unsporting behavior. A second yellow card results in a red card.

Red Card
A card given to a player for serious foul play or misconduct. The player is sent off the field and their team plays with one less player.

Cross
A pass made from the side of the pitch into the

center, usually aimed at creating a scoring opportunity.

Formation
The arrangement of players on the field, usually described by numbers indicating the positions of defenders, midfielders, and attackers.

Match
A game of football played between two teams, usually lasting 90 minutes, divided into two halves.

Goal
Scoring the ball into the opponent's net. A goal earns the team one point.

Understanding these basic football terms will help you follow the game better and appreciate the skills and strategies used by players like Cole Palmer. Keep exploring and learning, and soon you'll be a football expert yourself!

Acknowledgments

Thanking Those Who Helped with the Book

I would like to extend my heartfelt thanks to everyone who supported me in creating this book. A special thank you to Cole Palmer for sharing his inspiring story and allowing us to explore his journey. My gratitude also goes to my family and friends for their encouragement and assistance throughout this project. Your support and dedication made this book possible, and I am deeply appreciative.

About the Author

KLEIN B. SCOTT

KLEIN B. SCOTT is a passionate writer with a love for sports and storytelling. With a background in both journalism and creative writing, Scott has dedicated his career to bringing captivating and inspiring stories to readers of all ages. His interest in football and its stars has led him to write engaging biographies that highlight the achievements and journeys of remarkable athletes. Scott's goal is to inspire young readers through stories of perseverance, hard work, and dedication. When he's not writing, I "SCOTT" enjoys exploring new sports, spending time with family, and cheering on his favorite teams.

Printed in Great Britain
by Amazon

48197247R00046